# COLOSSAL CONTROVERSIES

## What was nailed to the cross?
## Are the dietary laws and the Sabbath now optional?

A BE KY Book ©

Robin Gould, D.R.E., LMFT

Cover design by Rubel Photography, Mt. Juliet, TN.

This booklet is a BEKY Book publication:
Books Encouraging the Kingdom of Yeshua.
www.bekybooks.com

ISBN-13: 9780996183932

# DEDICATION

*To my David,*

*because you believed in me.*

# CONTENTS

# GLOSSARY

**Asceticism** – severe self-discipline and avoidance of all forms of indulgence, typically for religious reasons.

**Didactic** – a manner of teaching or instructing which may be one-sided and can be overtly comprised of opinion, or even of a patronizing attitude.

**Doctrine** – a belief or set of beliefs held and taught by a church, political party, or other group.

**Dogmatic** – inclined to lay down principles as incontrovertibly true, but may be based on personal interpretation.

**Enigma** – a person or thing that is mysterious, puzzling, or difficult to understand.

**Ethnocentric** – evaluating other peoples and cultures according to the standards of one's own culture.

**Jewish Oral Law** – Jewish Oral Law traditionally is believed to have been passed down from Moses.

**Mishnah** – the codified Jewish Oral Law compiled and finally written down by Judah HaNasi around 200 A.D.; it is composed of six orders (sedarim) and sixty-three tractates.

**Paradigm** – an example or pattern of something; a model.

**Preemptive** – taken as a measure against something possible, anticipated, or feared; preventive; deterrent.

**Sanctification** – to be set apart for holy use; to be separate due to holy parameters or behavior that is compliant with holy standards and expectations.

**Supplant** – to supersede and replace or substitute, especially by force or treachery.

**Talmud** – the largest body of Jewish Law and commentary containing the Mishnah, Gemara, and Tosefta. It was not completed until the Medieval Period of history.

**Tome** – a book, especially a large, heavy, scholarly one.

**Torah** – The first five books of the Bible (Genesis, Exodus, Leviticus, Numbers, and Deuteronomy).

**Writ** – The physical legal declaration on paper; in the context of this booklet, a written legal declaration of the dissolution of a marriage.

# 1

# BOOK OR LETTER?

Information ardently debated is found in the Book of Colossians. Theologians differ widely on the message conveyed in the text, and much of this dispute is unknown to the general student of the Bible who seeks a quick understanding of New Testament documents for daily behavioral application. This booklet is designed for the serious and casual student alike, as truth is truth, and that which is provable is provable provided one is sufficiently armed with relevant historical, cultural, and linguistic understanding. This book explores two of the misunderstandings that emerge from a cursory survey of this letter, and it is for the sake of encouraging, motivating, and purifying.

Is the Book of Colossians really a book? No. *It is in a book*, but as a document itself, it is not a book. It is a letter. Is it a letter written *to* you? No. It is included in a book of other compiled letters *accessible to* you, but the letter, which was written approximately 50 A.D., was not written specifically to you.

This letter was not written to advise our modern

century of American issues within the contemporary governmental, social, religious, and political climate. It was a letter written to the people of Colossae to address the particular issues with which *they* travailed at that particular time. Further, this is not a stand-alone document. This letter was a response to a letter written to the author (Paul/*Shaul*) by the people of Colossae.

Does that mean that modern believers, when properly informed of the issues and language of the day, cannot decipher the letter's main points and glean wonderful principles to apply to our lives? Of course not. It's a valuable document. However, to accurately understand the content of this letter and the points it strives to make to its original audience requires some studious patience. The value of the letter is decreased by a didactic 20-minute pastoral sermon where a sentence or two is isolated and creatively morphed into an emotional plea promoting a generic, but well-intentioned principle.

This is not a rant against local pastors or Sunday school classes. Most often, congregational shepherds are genuine and earnest in their desire to be edifiers and encouragers. Even if their methods do not withstand the scrutiny of a true scholarly inquest, generally this is due to the erroneous education protocols of modern seminaries, not a reflection of the character or ability of the individual.

A student's job is to verify information and, as hard as it may be, step out of an ethnocentric church mentality. This myopic mindset has been embedded into us since we sat crossed legged on the carpet in children's church learning that the animals came onto the ark two by two (not entirely true) and that Lot's wife turned into a statue of salt (not entirely true either). We shall take our own portion, cut our own meat, and digest our own food. Students of the Word are not baby birds who need predigested material placed into their mouths. We are children of the King of Kings, and He speaks to us directly. Paul's letter to the people of Colossae has been the subject of years of doctrinal misunderstandings by sincere pastors educated in institutions that promote doctrinal positions rather than logical study paradigms. This letter has been a primary target for "verse plucking" in probably its most egregious form. Subsequently, this misunderstanding prevailed within the mainstream church and is just now being challenged in more vocal circles of those seeking truth. A scholarly exposition of this letter takes the entire letter into context, utilizing primary sources to illuminate the cultural reality at the time the letter was written.

Some of the basic rules of hermeneutics state:

> "Recognize the significance of the biblical language for proper interpretation...accustom yourself to the notion that there is a linguistic and cultural distance that separates us from the biblical text. While this distance should not be exaggerated, beware of reading into the Bible ideas that can be supported only from the English translation." (Kaiser, 1994, p. 63)

> "Do place priority on the attested and contemporary usage of words...writers depend on the way language is actually used in their time." (Kaiser, p. 64)

A frequent error of hermeneutics is "proof-texting." Here is how Kaiser describes this error:

> The proof-text model often relies on a naïve reading of the text. It may disregard the purpose for which the text was written, the historical conditioning in which it is set, and the genre convention that shaped it. Consequently, this method is vulnerable to allegorization, psychologization, spiritualization, and other forms of quick-and-easy adjustments of the scriptural words

to say what one wishes them to say in the contemporary scene, ignoring their intended purpose and usage as determined by context, grammar, and historical background." (Kaiser, p. 31-32)

In deference to the accepted rules of hermeneutics, let's take a look at the controversial letter in reference to its context, grammar, and historical background.

# 2

## CONTROVERSY #1: WHAT WAS NAILED TO THE CROSS? (COL. 2:14)

This verse in Colossians evokes a strong reaction due to the vital significance of that item, as indeed, whatever was nailed on the cross with the Messiah Yeshua (Jesus) had to be very important. The life, death, burial, and resurrection of the Son of the Almighty God was so imperative to the life and hope of this entire planet that all Truth hangs on it.

The discussion of what was nailed to the cross is found in Colossians 2:13-15:

> And you, who were dead in your trespasses and the uncircumcision of your flesh, God made alive together with him, having forgiven us all our trespasses, by canceling the record of debt which stood against us with its legal demands. This he set aside, **nailing it to the cross.** He disarmed the rulers and authorities and put them to open shame, by triumphing over them in him. (ESV)

Two ideas prevail of what was nailed to the cross. Before we explore further, let's examine what was *not* nailed to the cross.

## Theory #1: Was the Torah (law) nailed to the cross?

What was not nailed to the cross was the Torah. First, the description of what was nailed to the cross does not fit how the Heavenly Father describes the Torah. Let's insert the word Torah to illustrate:

> ...by canceling the Torah which stood against us with its legal demands. This he set aside, nailing it to the cross.

In contrast, the Torah is described in Psalm 119 (NIV):

### א Aleph

Blessed are those whose ways are blameless,
who walk according to the law of the Lord.
Blessed are those who keep his statutes
and seek him with all their heart—
They do no wrong but follow his ways.
You have laid down precepts that
are to be fully obeyed.
Oh, that my ways were steadfast
in obeying your decrees!
Then I would not be put to shame
when I consider all your commands.
I will praise you with an upright heart
as I learn your righteous laws.
I will obey your decrees; do not utterly forsake me.

### ב Beth

How can a young person stay on the path of purity?
By living according to your word.
I seek you with all my heart;
do not let me stray from your commands.
I have hidden your word in my heart
that I might not sin against you.
Praise be to you, Lord; teach me your decrees.

With my lips I recount all the laws
that come from your mouth.
I rejoice in following your statutes
as one rejoices in great riches.
I meditate on your precepts and consider your ways.
I delight in your decrees; I will not neglect your word.

## ג Gimel

Be good to your servant while I live,
that I may obey your word.
Open my eyes that I may see
wonderful things in your law.
I am a stranger on earth;
do not hide your commands from me.
My soul is consumed with longing
for your laws at all times.
You rebuke the arrogant, who are accursed,
those who stray from your commands.
Remove from me their scorn and contempt,
for I keep your statutes.
Though rulers sit together and slander me,
your servant will meditate on your decrees.
Your statutes are my delight; they are my counselors.

## ד Daleth

I am laid low in the dust; preserve my life
according to your word.
I gave an account of my ways and you answered me;
teach me your decrees.
Cause me to understand the way of your precepts,
that I may meditate on your wonderful deeds.
My soul is weary with sorrow;
strengthen me according to your word.
Keep me from deceitful ways;
be gracious to me and teach me your law.
I have chosen the way of faithfulness;
I have set my heart on your laws.
I hold fast to your statutes, Lord;
do not let me be put to shame.

I run in the path of your commands,
for you have broadened my understanding.

## ה **He**

Teach me, Lord, the way of your decrees,
that I may follow it to the end.
Give me understanding, so that I may keep your law
and obey it with all my heart.
Direct me in the path of your commands,
for there I find delight.
Turn my heart toward your statutes
and not toward selfish gain.
Turn my eyes away from worthless things;
preserve my life according to your word.
Fulfill your promise to your servant,
so that you may be feared.
Take away the disgrace I dread,
for your laws are good.
How I long for your precepts!
In your righteousness preserve my life.

## ו **Waw**

May your unfailing love come to me, Lord,
your salvation, according to your promise;
Then I can answer anyone who taunts me,
for I trust in your word.
Never take your word of truth from my mouth,
for I have put my hope in your laws.
I will always obey your law, for ever and ever.
I will walk about in freedom,
for I have sought out your precepts.
I will speak of your statutes before kings and will not be
put to shame, for I delight in your commands
because I love them.
I reach out for your commands, which I love,
that I may meditate on your decrees.

## ז Zayin

Remember your word to your servant,
for you have given me hope.
My comfort in my suffering is this:
Your promise preserves my life.
The arrogant mock me unmercifully,
but I do not turn from your law.
I remember, Lord, your ancient laws,
and I find comfort in them.
Indignation grips me because of the wicked,
who have forsaken your law.
Your decrees are the theme of my song
wherever I lodge.
In the night, Lord, I remember your name,
that I may keep your law.
This has been my practice: I obey your precepts.

## ח Heth

You are my portion, Lord;
I have promised to obey your words.
I have sought your face with all my heart;
be gracious to me according to your promise.
I have considered my ways and have
turned my steps to your statutes.
I will hasten and not delay to obey your commands.
Though the wicked bind me with ropes,
I will not forget your law.
At midnight I rise to give you thanks
for your righteous laws.
I am a friend to all who fear you,
to all who follow your precepts.
The earth is filled with your love, Lord;
teach me your decrees.

## ט Teth

Do good to your servant according to your word, Lord.
Teach me knowledge and good judgment,
for I trust your commands.

Before I was afflicted I went astray,
but now I obey your word.
You are good, and what you do is good;
teach me your decrees.
Though the arrogant have smeared me with lies,
I keep your precepts with all my heart.
Their hearts are callous and unfeeling,
but I delight in your law.
It was good for me to be afflicted
so that I might learn your decrees.
The law from your mouth is more precious to me
than thousands of pieces of silver and gold.

## ׳ Yodh

Your hands made me and formed me;
give me understanding to learn your commands.
May those who fear you rejoice when they see me,
for I have put my hope in your word.
I know, Lord, that your laws are righteous,
and that in faithfulness you have afflicted me.
May your unfailing love be my comfort,
according to your promise to your servant.
Let your compassion come to me that I may live,
for your law is my delight.
May the arrogant be put to shame for wronging me
without cause; but I will meditate on your precepts.
May those who fear you turn to me,
those who understand your statutes.
May I wholeheartedly follow your decrees, that I may
not be put to shame.

## כ Kaph

My soul faints with longing for your salvation,
but I have put my hope in your word.
My eyes fail, looking for your promise; I say,
"When will you comfort me?"
Though I am like a wineskin in the smoke,
I do not forget your decrees.
How long must your servant wait?

When will you punish my persecutors?
The arrogant dig pits to trap me, contrary to your law.
All your commands are trustworthy;
help me, for I am being persecuted without cause.
They almost wiped me from the earth,
but I have not forsaken your precepts.
In your unfailing love preserve my life,
that I may obey the statutes of your mouth.

## ל Lamedh

Your word, Lord, is eternal; it stands firm in the heavens.
Your faithfulness continues through all generations;
you established the earth, and it endures.
Your laws endure to this day, for all things serve you.
If your law had not been my delight,
I would have perished in my affliction.
I will never forget your precepts,
for by them you have preserved my life.
Save me, for I am yours;
I have sought out your precepts.
The wicked are waiting to destroy me,
but I will ponder your statutes.
To all perfection I see a limit,
but your commands are boundless.

## מ Mem

Oh, how I love your law! I meditate on it all day long.
Your commands are always with me
and make me wiser than my enemies.
I have more insight than all my teachers,
for I meditate on your statutes.
I have more understanding than the elders,
for I obey your precepts.
I have kept my feet from every evil path
so that I might obey your word.
I have not departed from your laws,
for you yourself have taught me.
How sweet are your words to my taste,
sweeter than honey to my mouth!

I gain understanding from your precepts;
therefore I hate every wrong path.

## נ Nun

Your word is a lamp for my feet, a light on my path.
I have taken an oath and confirmed it,
that I will follow your righteous laws.
I have suffered much; preserve my life, Lord,
according to your word.
Accept, Lord, the willing praise of my mouth,
and teach me your laws.
Though I constantly take my life in my hands,
I will not forget your law.
The wicked have set a snare for me,
but I have not strayed from your precepts.
Your statutes are my heritage forever;
they are the joy of my heart.
My heart is set on keeping your decrees
to the very end.

## ס Samekh

I hate double-minded people,
but I love your law.
You are my refuge and my shield;
I have put my hope in your word.
Away from me, you evildoers,
that I may keep the commands of my God!
Sustain me, my God, according to your promise,
and I will live; do not let my hopes be dashed.
Uphold me, and I will be delivered;
I will always have regard for your decrees.
You reject all who stray from your decrees,
for their delusions come to nothing.
All the wicked of the earth you discard like dross;
therefore I love your statutes.
My flesh trembles in fear of you;
I stand in awe of your laws.

## ע Ayin

I have done what is righteous and just;
do not leave me to my oppressors.
Ensure your servant's well-being;
do not let the arrogant oppress me.
My eyes fail, looking for your salvation,
looking for your righteous promise.
Deal with your servant according to your love
and teach me your decrees.
I am your servant; give me discernment
that I may understand your statutes.
It is time for you to act, Lord;
your law is being broken.
Because I love your commands more than gold,
more than pure gold, and because I consider
all your precepts right, I hate every wrong path.

## פ Pe

Your statutes are wonderful; therefore I obey them.
The unfolding of your words gives light;
it gives understanding to the simple.
I open my mouth and pant,
longing for your commands.
Turn to me and have mercy on me,
as you always do to those who love your name.
Direct my footsteps according to your word;
let no sin rule over me.
Redeem me from human oppression,
that I may obey your precepts.
Make your face shine on your servant
and teach me your decrees.
Streams of tears flow from my eyes,
for your law is not obeyed.

## צ Tsadhe

You are righteous, Lord, and your laws are right.
The statutes you have laid down are righteous;
they are fully trustworthy.

My zeal wears me out,
for my enemies ignore your words.
Your promises have been thoroughly tested,
and your servant loves them.
Though I am lowly and despised,
I do not forget your precepts.
Your righteousness is everlasting and your law is true.
Trouble and distress have come upon me,
but your commands give me delight.
Your statutes are always righteous;
give me understanding that I may live.

## ק Qoph

I call with all my heart; answer me, Lord,
and I will obey your decrees.
I call out to you; save me and I will keep your statutes.
I rise before dawn and cry for help;
I have put my hope in your word.
My eyes stay open through the watches of the night,
that I may meditate on your promises.
Hear my voice in accordance with your love;
preserve my life, Lord, according to your laws.
Those who devise wicked schemes are near,
but they are far from your law.
Yet you are near, Lord, and all your commands are true.
Long ago I learned from your statutes
that you established them to last forever.

## ר Resh

Look on my suffering and deliver me,
for I have not forgotten your law.
Defend my cause and redeem me;
preserve my life according to your promise.
Salvation is far from the wicked,
for they do not seek out your decrees.
Your compassion, Lord, is great;
preserve my life according to your laws.
Many are the foes who persecute me,
but I have not turned from your statutes.

I look on the faithless with loathing,
for they do not obey your word.
See how I love your precepts;
preserve my life, Lord,
in accordance with your love.
All your words are true;
all your righteous laws are eternal.

## שׁ Sin and Shin

Rulers persecute me without cause,
but my heart trembles at your word.
I rejoice in your promise like one who finds great spoil.
I hate and detest falsehood but I love your law.
Seven times a day I praise you for your righteous laws.
Great peace have those who love your law,
and nothing can make them stumble.
I wait for your salvation, Lord,
and I follow your commands.
I obey your statutes, for I love them greatly.
I obey your precepts and your statutes,
for all my ways are known to you.

## ת Taw

May my cry come before you, Lord;
give me understanding according to your word.
May my supplication come before you;
deliver me according to your promise.
May my lips overflow with praise,
for you teach me your decrees.
May my tongue sing of your word,
for all your commands are righteous.
May your hand be ready to help me,
for I have chosen your precepts.
I long for your salvation, Lord,
and your law gives me delight.
Let me live that I may praise you,
and may your laws sustain me.
I have strayed like a lost sheep.
Seek your servant,

for I have not forgotten your commands.

Does it sound like the Torah is against believers in Yeshua? Clearly not. In fact, not only is the Torah not against us, it is *of* Him and *for* us. Does the Father curse His children by giving them a law that is against them? The Father loves His children, and He provides them with instructions to bless them and to bring them to prosperity. This favor from the Torah is found in a few other places.

If you fully obey the Lord your God and carefully follow all his commands I give you today, the Lord your God will set you high above all the nations on earth. All these blessings will come on you and accompany you if you obey the Lord your God: You will be blessed in the city and blessed in the country. The fruit of your womb will be blessed, and the crops of your land and the young of your livestock—the calves of your herds and the lambs of your flocks. Your basket and your kneading trough will be blessed. You will be blessed when you come in and blessed when you go out. The Lord will grant that the enemies who rise up against you will be defeated before you. They will come at you from one direction but flee from you in seven. The Lord will send a blessing on your barns and on everything you put your hand to. The Lord your God will bless you in the land he is giving you. The Lord will establish you as his holy people, as he promised you on oath, if you keep the commands of the Lord your God and walk in obedience to him. Then all the peoples on earth will see that you are called by the name of the Lord, and they will fear you. The Lord will grant you abundant prosperity—in the fruit of your womb, the young of your livestock and the crops of your ground—in the land he swore to your ancestors to give you. The Lord will open the heavens, the storehouse of his bounty, to send rain on your land in season and to bless all the work of your hands. You will lend to many nations but will borrow from none. The Lord will make you the head, not the tail. If you pay attention to the commands of the Lord your God that I give you this day and carefully follow them, you will always be at the top, never at the bottom. Do not turn aside from any of the commands I give you today, to the right or to the left, following other gods and serving them." (Deut. 28: 1-14 NIV)

Now what I am commanding you today is not too difficult for you or beyond your reach. It is not up in heaven, so that you have to ask, "Who will ascend into heaven to get it and proclaim it to us so we may obey it?" Nor is it beyond the sea, so that you have to ask, "Who will cross the sea to get it and proclaim it to us so we may obey it?" No, the word is very near you; it is in your mouth and in your heart so you may obey it. See, I set before you today life and prosperity, death and destruction. For I command you today to love the Lord your God, to walk in obedience to him, and to keep his commands, decrees and laws; then you will live and increase, and the Lord your God will bless you in the land you are entering to possess. (Deut. 30:11-16 NIV)

Again, are the Father's words conveying that the Torah is a handbook of busywork to placate the people until the "real" God arrives to make everything right? No, quite the contrary. The Torah is a set of instructions to bless His children. The Torah guided as the remedy for all that is discordant before anything became discordant, and still does. The Most High God is never caught unaware; He was not backed into a corner with a "plan B" because people ruined "plan A." Nor is the Torah a penal code thrust upon unsuspecting slaves by a judge preemptively punishing with instructions. He did not set His children up for failure, only to recant later with a new set of "fair" instructions. The Father did not recruit humans to police, but rather He birthed children to parent.

**Theory #2: Was it the Talmud that was nailed to the cross?**

The other proposal is that what was "nailed to the cross" was the dogmatic additions to the Jewish oral law. The Jewish oral law of the First Century was traditional and historical customs of how to walk out the written commandments. This orally-transmitted law, which was written down around 200 A.D., was called the Mishnah. By the medieval period, the Mishnah had accumulated and morphed into an encyclopedic set of tomes called the *Talmud*. In fact, many Christians do not know the difference between the Torah and the Mishnah or *Talmud*, often considering them one in the same. Just to review, the Torah is the first five books of the Bible (Genesis, Exodus, Leviticus, Numbers, and Deuteronomy).

While the *Talmud* is full of insightful commentary that can be helpful, it was not completed until the medieval period, far after the cross. Any discussion concerning the cross and the *Talmud* is not historically relevant even though the Talmud's base text (along with the Torah) is the Mishnah, or Jewish oral law. The Mishnah, which contains rulings that were debated in the First Century, also contains traditions [1].

1. For a brief history of the Jewish Oral Law (Mishnah) and Talmud, see S. Creeger's BEKY Book

Some of the rulings of the oral law Yeshua spoke against, primarily because the enforcement of them supplanted the written commandments of the Father. Yeshua sometimes agreed with points of oral law, but he reproved those who skirted the actual written commandments or insisted on its observance in place

26

of the weightier matters of mercy and justice. In Yeshua's teaching, oral law was to be a vehicle for observing the written law, not a substitution for it.

What was not nailed to the cross was the additions to the oral law, the *Talmud*. Clearly Yeshua hated these additions when they supplanted obedience to the actual commandments, but the letter to the Colossians does not even remotely suggest that these man-made laws were what was nailed to the cross, nor is there any prophecy anywhere in the entire Bible that this would happen.

It was never prophesied that any additions to oral law would need to be conquered by a sacrificial death. The Talmudic additions exceeding the oral law were never acknowledged by the Father as being enforceable law, nor did it even exist yet, so why would it require the death of His Son to remove its power? It was never prophesied or reported that the Torah or the *Talmud* would be what we were cleansed or delivered from by blood.

In John 1:29, John states, "Behold *the Lamb of God who taketh away the sin of the world*." (KJV) He does not state; "*Behold the Lamb of God who taketh away the law of God*."

In Matthew 26:28 Jesus himself said that his blood was shed "*for the remission of sin*." He did not say that his blood was shed "*for the remission of the law*." 1 John 3:5 says "*He was manifested to take away our sins*." John did not say; "*He was manifested to take away the law*." Isaiah prophesied that what would be taken away was sin. Isaiah 53:10 says that He will be "*an offering for sin*." 1 John 1:7 says that His blood "*cleanses us from all sin*." Revelation 1:5 says He "*washed us from our sins in His own blood*."

It makes no logical sense, nor can it be verified by scripture that dogmatic additions to the Torah, nor the Torah itself was nailed to the cross. So, what was?

The scriptural text suggests that what was nailed to the cross was the list of debts/penalties that repentant sinners acquired through transgression of the Torah, which is the definition of sin (see 1 John 3:4). By extension, this covers the resulting "writ of divorce" (which detailed the transgressions) that was handed by the Father to the House of Israel for violation of the covenants. This "writ" is what stood against us. This writ invoked "the law of the husband" which is detailed in Deuteronomy.

> If a man marries a woman who becomes displeasing to him because he finds something indecent about her, and he writes her a certificate of divorce, gives it to her and sends her from his house, and if after she leaves his house she becomes the wife of another man, and her second husband dislikes her and writes her a certificate of divorce, gives it to her and sends her from his house, or if he dies, then *her first husband, who divorced her, is not allowed to marry her again* after she has been defiled. That would be detestable in the eyes of the Lord. Do not bring sin upon the land the Lord your God is giving you as an inheritance. (Deut. 24:1-4 NIV)

Biblical history teaches that the twelve tribes split into two Kingdoms; the Southern Kingdom (Judah and Benjamin) who remained near the temple, and the Northern Kingdom (the remaining ten tribes) who followed Jereboam north, where a counterfeit temple was built and used. (I Kings)

Sometimes these two groups are referred to as respective houses, namely the House of Judah and the House of Israel. The House of Judah had a few good kings, and thus had periods of repentance and reverence to God, but the House of Israel had no good kings. While both Judah and Israel went astray, Israel violated the covenant more severely and never repented, despite many opportunities to do so. Therefore, God divorced the House of Israel. (Jeremiah 3:8)

The House of Israel remained in the north and became homogenized with the gentiles in those areas. The House of Israel was subject to the law of the husband that was invoked upon Himself divorcing her, and her subsequent harlotry. The House of Israel is now prevented from ever remarrying her Creator, and yet He declares He will marry her in a new covenant. Thus, the old covenant has to be severed because in it is the law of the husband that stands against this future marriage.

Yeshua in Matthew 15:24 says He came only for lost sheep of the Northern Kingdom (the House of Israel). This statement confuses so many Christians that they simply ignore this proclamation, for they have no explanation, though with the historical context, it is easy to see what He meant. His first coming was specifically designed to accomplish, by death, release for those who needed to be brought back into covenant. The divorced House of Israel was held back by the permanent shunning due to the Law of the Husband.

Yeshua did not become an alternative to the covenant; He became their invitation back in. Refer to Deuteronomy 24. What was a condition that severs marital law? The death of the husband. In Romans 7, Paul discusses this amazing mystery now solved by quoting the Torah on this matter. When the husband dies, all marital connections, and in the case of the law of the husband, all prohibitions (such as never being eligible to marry that former spouse), are severed. The shunned ones are now released from the law of the husband.

> Or do you not know, brethren (for I
> am speaking to those who know the
> law), that the law has jurisdiction over
> a person as long as he lives? For the
> married woman is bound by law to her
> husband while he is living; but if her
> husband dies, she is released from the

law concerning the husband. So then, if while her husband is living she is joined to another man, she shall be called an adulteress; but if her husband dies, she is free from the law, so that she is not an adulteress though she is joined to another man. (Romans 7:1-3 NAS)

Some who have not learned Torah law on marriage and divorce have misunderstood Paul's words to the Romans and thought that Paul was saying that covenant people were released from the entire law itself, rather than just the law of the husband, to which Paul is referring. This is why he qualifies the reader only if they *know the law* (vs 1). He goes on to describe that the born again death of the ex-wife and the physical death of the husband accomplishes the miracle of even the unredeemable to be redeemed.

The outcome of this act is nothing short of astonishing. In nailing this writ to the cross, the law remained intact. Heaven and Earth have not passed away, yet just as Yeshua declared, it was only then that even the smallest letter of the law would remain intact, and was miraculously upheld WHILE those permanently shunned were purchased back by virtue of an act of intelligence we could never even fathom.

2. In rabbinic thought, there are two manifestations of the Messiah, the Messiah ben Yosef, the suffering servant, and Messiah ben David, the ruling king. (Jacobs, J. & Buttenwieser, M., 1906)

Essentially, He came to release the House of Israel from the utter and complete destruction from the "famine" (allegorically and in the pattern illustrated as Messiah Ben Yosef [2] as the suffering servant. His second coming will not require a death, but rather wields an authority over all (allegorically and in the pattern illustrated as Messiah Ben David) "to rule over the throne of His father David" (all 12 tribes). Since the death of the husband released all marital laws, by extension this would include the prohibition of a resumed covenant due to the divorce detailed in the Law of the Husband as Paul explains in Romans 7. By accomplishing this, Yeshua reunited the specific group He says He came for, reversing their status from being lost to being found.

Verse 15 states "and having spoiled principalities and powers, he made a shew of them openly, triumphing over them in it." Traditional church theology asserts that Yeshua was demonstrating that those who still taught Torah were in error, and He was publicly rebuking them by His death. This makes no sense. There are no texts that say He came to do away with the law because it would contradict the assertion that the new covenant would be written on our hearts. In fact, He confirms this in Matthew 5:17, "Think not that I have come to destroy the law…" John 1:1-3 states that He was the Word of God, with God from the beginning, and through Him all things were made. Why would He come to undo or destroy what He made? The "mystery of the Gospel" which is the death and resurrection of the husband to release the House of Israel from "the law of the husband," all while upholding the law, expresses a love beyond our human measure.

# 3

## CONTROVERSY #2: CAN WE JUDGE ON MATTERS OF TORAH OBSERVANCE? (COL 2:16)

Chapter Two in the letter from Paul to the Colossians also has some hot spots for debate if read with a filter erected from reading the second half of the book first, rather than the other way around, which happens often. When you write letters, do you segment the content into chapters? No? Do you think Paul segmented his thoughts in this letter into chapters? No, he did not. Chapters were added by the translators. Bear in mind that often these man-made parameters can interrupt the stream of thought of the writer and reduce the clarity of the content for the reader. Let me give you an example of this tampering using a letter that I wrote to my cousin.

```
Dear Whitney,

Chapter 1

It is with great joy that I
send you this letter because
I finally ended up finding that
picnic area you suggested. It was
beautiful. The facilities were
```

open and parking was abundant. It really solved our problem of where to have our faculty appreciation day. I appreciate your suggestion. Thank you! I can see why you reserved it for our family reunion and I am not surprised everyone had a great time! I wish I had not been out of country then…I would have loved to attend.

**Chapter 2**

Family is significant and it is important that we look out for each other. We must go that extra mile and show up for each other. When people don't do that, we all lose. The opportunity to be a blessing is forfeited and the opportunity to be blessed is missed. I wish this was a more common way of thinking.

**Chapter 3**

Hoping that you have a successful move and that it is not too stressful for you. Be strong in your new town and know that in time you will get used to it and find a supportive group of friends.

Love, Robin

Now read those chapters separately and out of order. If you started with chapter two, you might perceive that I am rebuking my cousin and our family for not being supportive enough of each other. If you then added chapter three you might wonder if this person was leaving due to family hostility in pursuit of support. Without the context of chapter one, you will no doubt read into the letter a tone that does not exist. I include this example to make the point of reading an entire letter, knowing the people writing and receiving, and being sufficiently acquainted with their language before feeling confident that you understand the direction and agenda of the letter.

People are people. Paul is no exception. He wrote a letter and sent it to a targeted audience. He expected them to read the entire letter, keeping middle paragraphs in context with earlier paragraphs, as well as keeping the entire letter in context with his expertise in Torah.

Sadly, that has not occurred, and a damaging irony has emerged. The very opposite message of what Paul was writing has been credited to him. It would most certainly grieve his heart monumentally to see how his words are being portrayed.

The commonly used translation of Col. 2:16-17:

> Let no man therefore judge you in meat,
> or in drink, or in respect of a holyday,
> or of the new moon, or of the Sabbath
> days which are a shadow of things to
> come; but the substance is of Messiah.
> (KJV)

This translation, combined with lack of knowledge of the regional spiritual practices from which the new believers emerged, can lead to misunderstanding.

Who were the Colossians? It is well documented that the people of Colossae were ascetics. Asceticism holds that a person could not be spiritual unless he or she was in a state of denial of bodily pleasure and imposing harsh treatment of the body. Have you emerged from a background of an ascetic practice to the point of harming your body? If not, read this letter as it is meant

35

to be read, which is to the Colossians struggling with the embedded and practiced societal rules of this harsh bodily treatment to please their former gods. This is at odds with the Torah concept of sanctification (which is achieved through obedience to the commandments) and justification (redemption, which is achieved through the blood of the Messiah). Our Father is *never* pleased with self-harm.

By contrast to ascetic practices, the festival days of the LORD are often times of feasting and making merry with celebration and wonderful fellowship. The festivals of the Lord would be confusing to those who see suffering as a way to prove loyalty. These new believers certainly were misunderstood by their former peers, for we read Paul encouraging them in this way earlier in the letter.

> Once you were alienated from God and were enemies in your minds because of your evil behavior. But now he has reconciled you by Christ's physical body through death to present you holy in his sight, without blemish and free from accusation (Col. 1:21-22 NIV)

In other words, the ex-pagans of Colossae had previously been alienated from the Father because of their evil works, but now they have received peace by His sacrifice, and been set apart (brought into the commandments; The Torah), without any offense against the Father...they had been washed clean.

Now that we have established to whom Paul writes, what is the letter about? The point redundantly reiterated in this letter is a clear warning to these new believers against the beliefs and ways of man above the commandments of the Father.

> For I want you to know how great a struggle I have on your behalf and for those who are at Laodicea, and for all those who have not personally

seen my face, that their hearts may be encouraged, having been knit together in love, and attaining to all the wealth that comes from the full assurance of understanding, resulting in a true knowledge of God's mystery, that is, Christ Himself, in whom are hidden all the treasures of wisdom and knowledge. I say this so that no one will delude you with persuasive argument. For even though I am absent in body, nevertheless I am with you in spirit, rejoicing to see your good discipline and the stability of your faith in Christ. Therefore as you have received Christ Jesus the Lord, so walk in Him, having been firmly rooted and now being built up in Him and established in your faith, just as you were instructed, and overflowing with gratitude. See to it that no one takes you captive through philosophy and empty deception, according to the tradition of men, according to the elementary principles of the world, rather than according to Christ. (Col. 2:1-8 NAS)

Paul continues in his encouragement for these new believers to persevere in their obedience to the Torah and to abandon their former religion and religious ways.

For in Him all the fullness of Deity dwells in bodily form, and in Him you have been made complete, and He is the head over all rule and authority; and in Him you were also circumcised with a circumcision made without hands, in the removal of the body of the flesh by the circumcision of Christ; having been buried with Him in baptism, in which you were also raised up with Him through faith in the working of God, who raised

Him from the dead. When you were dead in your transgressions and the uncircumcision of your flesh, He made you alive together with Him, having forgiven us all our transgressions, having canceled out the certificate of debt consisting of decrees against us, which was hostile to us; and He has taken it out of the way, having nailed it to the cross. When He had disarmed the rulers and authorities, He made a public display of them, having triumphed over them through Him. Therefore no one is to act as your judge in regard to food or drink or in respect to a festival or a new moon or a Sabbath day — things which are a mere shadow of what is to come; but the substance belongs to Christ. Let no one keep defrauding you of your prize by delighting in self-abasement and the worship of the angels, taking his stand on visions he has seen, inflated without cause by his fleshly mind, and not holding fast to the head, from whom the entire body, being supplied and held together by the joints and ligaments, grows with a growth which is from God. (Col. 2:9-19 NAS)

## What are these elementary principles/rudiments of the world?

20."Wherefore if ye be dead with Christ from the **rudiments of the world**, why, as though living in the world, are ye subject to its ordinances; 21."Do not handle! Do not taste! Do not touch!"? 22. These are all destined to perish with use, because they are based on human commands and teachings. 23. Such regulations indeed have an appearance of wisdom, with their self-imposed worship,

their false humility and their harsh
treatment of the body, but they lack any
value in managing the fleshly desires."
(Col. 2:20-23 NIV)

These regulations are not the Torah dietary laws,
observance of the Sabbath, Holy days, or New Moons.
Quite the contrary. They are specifically identified by
Paul as "the world's ordinances" (vs 20) and "human
commands and teachings" (vs 22). Further, it cannot be
suggested that God's laws are "self-imposed worship"
or "false humility." Nor are His food laws or Sabbaths to
be considered harsh treatment of the body. If anything,
consuming unclean items is a harsh treatment of the
body, according to science. A day of rest is anything but
harsh treatment of the body. Can we accuse His Torah
of "having no value in producing good fruit"? Of course
not.

These rudiments termed as "human commands" are
the man-made rudiments of asceticism, the world these
people were formerly enslaved to. "Hey, you are no
longer part of that group, so why do you care what they
are saying?"

There are many other translational issues in this passage,
where the translation simply does not match the original
text...the actual Greek words being used. It is important
to understand this. Let's form the definition of the word
"body" in this letter.

Col. 1:18+24

18. And he is the head of the **body**, the
church/assembly; he is the beginning
and the firstborn from among the dead,
so that in everything he might have the
supremacy. (NIV)

24. And I rejoice in the sufferings which
are for your sakes; and, in my flesh, I fill
up the deficiency in the afflictions of the

Messiah, in behalf of His **body** which is the assembly.

The Body of Messiah is the assembly, which is the gathering of believers. The word body in Greek is *soma*.

The Body of Messiah = the ASSEMBLY of Believers

Paul is talking to the ex-pagans/ascetics, instructing them to know who they are; SET APART, HOLY, no longer following the doctrines of men. He is reminding them that now they are no longer in the group of "evil doers" (those who practice lawlessness), and that they have been given peace. They are grafted into the family [3].

Let no man therefore judge you in meat, or in drink, or in respect of an holyday, or of the new moon, or of the Sabbath days: 2:17 Which are a shadow of things to come; but the body of Messiah (assembly). (Col. 2:16)

Don't let who judge? He is still speaking about those with whom they were formerly a part; the pagans/ascetics. When "judge" also appears in verse 16, as in "Let no one therefore judge you..," the context indicates the real meaning: "Let no (pagan or worldly person) therefore judge you…" since "therefore" is a conjunction indicating the stream of thought which is being followed. There was no punctuation in the original texts; punctuation was added by the translators.

Many Bibles, including the KJV, read:

16 Let no man therefore judge you in meat, or in drink, or in respect of an holyday, or of the new moon, or of the Sabbath days: 17 Which are a shadow of things to come; but the body is of Christ. (Col. 2:16-17, KJV)

3. The Olive tree symbolize Israel. "Grafted in" means a branch sown into the tree becomes a living, growing, thriving part of the tree..

The word *is* in verse 17 is in italics. This means that this word did not appear in the original text, but was *added by the translators*. Some translations even blatantly change the word "body" in that verse to read "substance" or "reality." The NIV outright adds the words "belongs to." Earlier passages in this same letter provide the context and wording without dispute. This was about the assembly, which, according to this letter, is the body of Messiah. The word for body **soma** (*somatos* = plural) is used again.

When you add the word *is*, you can no longer use the word "body" consistently with its usage throughout the entire rest of the letter. This is why some translations outright changed the word "body" to accommodate the added verb "is". The scholarly goal is to refrain from altering the written word to accommodate the verbs we have added ourselves. Translational bias can lead the reader into forming an opinion the translator held or wanted others to hold.

Remove the added word "is," and see what it reads.

> Let no man therefore judge you in
> eating, or in drinking, in part of an
> holyday, or the new moon, or the
> Sabbath days which are a shadow of
> things to come but the body of Messiah.
> (Col 2:16)

Adding the word "is" significantly alters the text. It changes the proper use of the word "but" and causes it to be read as a "contrasting" coordinating conjunction rather than a "connecting with exception" coordinating conjunction.

Compare two uses of the word "but":

- To suggest a contrast that is unexpected in light of the first clause: "Joey lost a fortune in the stock market, but he still seems able to live quite comfortably."
- To connect two ideas with the meaning of "with

the exception of" (and then the second word takes over as subject): "There is nobody you should trust but God."

Take out everything after "Let no man judge" and fast forward to the word "but," and see if it makes sense as it is written without the added word "is." If we are using the word "body" consistently with usage found in the rest of the letter, it SHOULD make sense with the middle content removed.

- "Let no man therefore judge you but the body *is* of Messiah. "
- "Let no man therefore judge you but the body of Messiah. "

In short, using "body" consistently with the use of it throughout this letter, the basic instruction is:

**"Let no one judge you but the assembly."**

This isn't instructing that no one is allowed to provide judgment on these matters. It is instructing who is qualified to judge in matters regarding the feasts/appointed times.

**Q.** Who can judge?

**A.** The assembly only.

**Q.** Why can they judge?

**A.** Because they know the Messiah!

Put this together so far.

> Let no man therefore judge you in eating, or in drinking, in part of an holyday, or the new moon, or the Sabbath days which are a shadow of things to come but the body of Messiah. (Col 2:16)

Notice the replacement of the words "food" and "drink" with the accurate translation "eating" (brosei) and "drinking" (posei). Paul is not speaking of clean or unclean food or drink. In fact, there is no such thing as an unclean drink. These words are in their active form in the original Greek. This instruction is not about *what* you eat or drink...this is about *if* you eat or drink. This is about fasting.

> Let no man therefore judge you in eating, or in drinking, in respect to a holyday, or the new moon, or the Sabbath days but the body of Messiah. (Col. 2:16)

Paul heartens the believers by encouraging them not to succumb to those pagans' judgment of them. He instructs them to feast on the festivals of the Torah that call for it and to keep the Torah commandments, including the holy days [4]. He tells them to continue observing the New Moon, and to resist the ascetic practices that push them toward fasting. The only people qualified to speak of such matters will be in the assembly...those in Messiah.

4. The three main feasts of the seven are Passover, Pentecost, and Tabernacles

# 4

# SHADOWS: THINGS TO COME

The irony of using the verses to suggest that the dietary laws, the Sabbath, the feasts, and the New Moons are optional (a mere shadow and no more) is that the verse, when taken in context with the rest of the letter, does just the opposite. Rather, it is an admonition of *not* letting the world *talk you out of observing them* or even influence *how* you observe them because these are a shadow of what is to come. Consider that; a shadow of *things to come*. Why would it be argued that we are no longer to practice things that are an outline of the future? These aren't events to leave behind the cross. On the contrary, they are *real because of the cross*, and because of the cross they are now *for* the Colossians who had repented!

Paul is not saying "Don't let the people who know Yeshua and are observing the Torah judge you if you *don't* obey the commandments." On the contrary, he is saying *do not* let the pagans (or even the nonbelieving Pharisees for that matter) who don't know Yeshua judge when or how you *do* obey the commandments! Only those who know Yeshua can judge because they understand the scope of what is happening. After all, this is a shadow of the future! The Messiah returns only for His own. Do you cease doing things that point to something that has not yet happened? Why would it make sense that people prior to the cross would be the only ones to observe them when they are an outline of the future?

Grace is free. It can't be earned through harsh treatment of the body. Our flesh will not be subdued because we punish it, but rather, because we submit it to the Father and rely on the Messiah to transform us. Paul is saying that the Colossians have been "washed clean" and are no longer part of the group that adheres to the "rudiments of the world."

> And you, being dead in your sins and the uncircumcision of your flesh, hath he quickened together with him, having forgiven you all trespasses; 14. Blotting out the handwriting of ordinances that was against us, which was contrary to us, and took it out of the way, nailing it to his cross... (Col. 2:13-14 KJV)

The Colossians are to listen to outsiders no longer. Their debts were paid when the Messiah took their penalty away. Washed clean and grafted in, they are to take their counsel from those who know and love the Messiah. They are to compare themselves only to the Torah, and not to the world.

The Sabbath, feast days, and dietary laws were never the "rudiments of the world." Paul is saying that believers are no longer to be judged by non-Torah standards because they are no longer part of the non-Torah world. They have been set apart and made clean. They are to be judged by Torah standards. They have changed groups. Make no mistake, these people were grafted in, set apart, and washed clean. They were *brought into* covenant, not *delivered from* covenant. They were receiving a letter from Paul  to remind them that the commandments set them apart. The blood washed them clean. *This is the good news.*

The good news is not that it was finally acknowledged that God's laws were unfair, and thus, no longer applicable. How could that be good news? In fact, the suggestion that His perfect Torah is anything other than perfect is a rudiment of the world!

The festivals that outsiders may not judge are the Feasts of Israel. The word "feasts" (*heortēs* in Greek/*moadim* in Hebrew) when discussing the seven feasts of God means "appointed times." He calls them "holy convocations" which is the Hebrew word *miqra*, meaning "rehearsal." He calls them **His** feasts and **your** rehearsals. Paul isn't identifying these events as being a "mere shadow." He parenthetically mentions the futurist nature of these things as being an outline of the future to *underscore its importance*. Paraphrase: Who cares what the unbelieving world thinks about these feasts? It is more than worth it! These are the *outline of the future*...and the future is for the washed ones!!

A person who does not know the Messiah could never understand the celebration of His death. Believers rejoice in these festivals because this is our hope. This was the advice the Colossians received. Do not let people who do not know Yeshua sway you in any way in regard to your celebrating. Paul was not writing that any of these feasts, the Sabbath, or the dietary laws are optional.

> Let no man therefore judge you in
> eating, or in drinking, in respect to
> a holyday, or the new moon, or the
> Sabbath days but the body of Messiah
> for these are an outline of what is to
> come. (Col. 2:16)

Uncovering the secrets of these verses to get to their real meaning is a journey of enigmas, for with very little exposition, the truth tumbles out so easily. Proper translation does not pit Paul against the Messiah, or the Messiah against the Father. It is one seamless book with one single message and no recanting. Hopefully, this small book on only two of these colossal controversies in the letter from Paul to the Colossians has inspired greater faith in the perfect plan of the Father.

# REVIEW STUDY QUESTIONS

1. Is the "Book of Colossians" really a book? If not, what is it?


2. Who were the Colossians? What did they believe before they converted to the ways of the Torah?


3. Is the Torah described as a negative thing in the Psalms? If not, what are some words used to describe it? How about in Deuteronomy 28:1?


4. What are the two houses called that the 12 tribes split into after King Solomon's reign?


5. To whom was Paul speaking specifically in Romans 7:1? What is the qualifying factor the reader of this letter must have according to Paul?


6. The original letters in the New Testament were not segmented into chapters. What are some possible errors that could be made by the readers if they don't know that?


7. Are God's laws considered "rudiments of the world"? If not, why?

8. What is the difference between sanctification and justification?


9. What is the biblical definition of lawlessness? (Hint: 1 John 3:4)


10. Is a shadow of things "to come" about the future or the past? Explain.

# REFERENCES

Kaiser, W. 1994. An introduction to biblical hermeneutics: the search for meaning. Grand Rapids: Zondervan.

Jacobs, J. & Buttenwieser, M. 1906. Messiah. Jewish Encyclopedia. Retrieved May 12, 2016 from http://www.jewishencyclopedia.com/articles/10729-messiah.

Daniel Gregg, *The Good News of Mĕssiah*, first published by the author in 2011 through the third edition in 2017. Fourth edition forthcoming in 2017: www.torahtimes.org.

# ABOUT
# THE AUTHOR

The author holds a Ph.D. in Religious Education and a Master's degree in Marriage and Family Therapy. With a background in both spiritual study and relational healing, she writes from a place of compassion, clarity, and deep respect for the human experience. Dr. Gould's work explores themes of faith, growth, and emotional stability.

# OTHER BOOKS BY THE AUTHOR

All titles are available on Amazon.

- *Colossal Controversies, 2016*

- *Divorce and Remarriage in the Bible, 2016*

- *Peter's Vision, 2016*

- *First Century Words Revealed to Twenty-First Century Believers, 2017*

- *The Forgiveness Tarts, 2018*

# ACKNOWLEDGEMENTS

Thank you to Daniel Gregg for taking the time so many years ago to help me understand the Colossian culture on this matter. Your bible translation was extremely helpful as a study tool for this book.